Other golf books published by Exley:
The Crazy World of Golf   Golf Address Book
The Fanatic's Guide to Golf   Golf Jokes

Published simultaneously in 1992 by Exley Publications Ltd in Great
Britain, and Exley Giftbooks in the USA.
First published in Great Britain in 1991 by Exley Publications Ltd.
Copyright © Helen Exley 1991
Reprinted 1991
Third, fourth and fifth printings 1992
Sixth printing 1993.
ISBN 1-85015-257-8
A copy of the CIP data is available from the British Library on request.
Designed by Pinpoint Design Company.
Edited by Helen Exley.
Printed in Hungary

Picture credits:
Nick Birch, photography/Sarah Baddiel of Golfiana, "The Book
Gallery", B12 Grays Antique Market, Davies Mews, London W1: 7, 15,
16, 19, 21, 27, 28, 31, 38, 42, 45, 47, 48, 55, 58, 61; Mary Evans
Picture Library: 52-53; Exley Publications: Front cover, 5, 9, 10, 25,
51, 57; Fotomas: 14, 29, 37, 39, 59; Hulton-Deutsch Collection: 44;
Private Collection (J.E.M.), Paris: 35, Lynn Tait Gallery: 22-23.
Acknowledgements: Extracts from Golfing: A Duffer's Dictionary by
Henry Beard and Roy McKie are reprinted by permission of the
publishers, Methuen (London) and Workman Publishing (New York).
Extracts from The Cheat's Guide to Golf by Colin Bowles, Published by
Angus & Robertson, are reprinted by courtesy of Curtis Brown (Aust)
Pty Ltd. Extracts from Bluff Your Way in Golf by Peter Gammond,
published by Ravette Books Limited, are reprinted by kind permission
of the publisher.

Exley Publications Ltd, 16 Chalk Hill, Watford, Herts WD1 4BN,
United Kingdom.
Exley Giftbooks, 359 East Main Street, Suite 3D, Mount Kisco,
NY 10549, USA.

GOLF
QUOTATIONS

A COLLECTION OF
STYLISH PICTURES AND THE
BEST GOLF QUOTES

- ◆ -

EDITED BY
HELEN EXLEY

▤EXLEY
MT. KISCO, NEW YORK • WATFORD, UK

"Golf is a game whose aim is to hit a very small ball into an even smaller hole, with weapons singularly ill-designed for the purpose."

SIR WINSTON CHURCHILL

"I'd give up golf if I didn't have so many sweaters."

BOB HOPE

"Willis' Rule of Golf: You can't lose an old golf ball."

JOHN WILLIS

"My handicap? Woods and irons."

CHRIS CODIROLI

"Practice Tee: The place where golfers go to convert a nasty hook into a wicked slice."

HENRY BEARD AND ROY MCKIE
from "Golfing - A Duffer's Dictionary"

"Golf increases the blood pressure, ruins the disposition, spoils the digestion, induces neurasthenia, hurts the eyes, callouses the hands, ties kinks in the nervous system, debauches the morals, drives men to drink or homicide, breaks up the family, turns the ductless glands into internal warts, corrodes the pneumo-gastric nerve, breaks off the edges of the vertebrae, induces spinal meningitis and progressive mendacity, and starts angina pectoris."

DR A. S. LAMB

– ◆ –

"Golf is a game where guts, stick-to-itiveness and blind devotion will always net you absolutely nothing but an ulcer."

TOMMY BOLT

– ◆ –

Golf: "A game in which a ball one and a half inches in diameter is placed on a ball 8,000 miles in diameter.
The object is to hit the small ball but not the larger."

JOHN CUNNINGHAM

– ◆ –

"Golf is a good walk spoiled."

MARK TWAIN

— ♦ —

"Daddy," said the bright child, accompanying her father on a round of golf, "why mustn't the ball go into the little hole?"

HERBERT V. PROCHNOW and HERBERT V. PROCHNOW JNR

— ♦ —

"Handicap: An allocation of strokes on one or more holes that permits two golfers of very different ability to do equally poorly on the same course."

HENRY BEARD AND ROY MCKIE
from "Golfing - A Duffer's Dictionary"

— ♦ —

"Golf is a game in which you yell Fore, shoot six, and write down five."

PAUL HARVEY
from "Golf Digest"

— ♦ —

THE MISERY OF GOLF

"Watching The Masters on CBS is like attending a church service. Announcers speak in hushed, pious tones, as if to convince us that something of great meaning and historical importance is taking place. What we are actually seeing is grown men hitting little balls with sticks."

TOM GILMORE
from "The San Francisco Chronicle"

— ♦ —

"I've just discovered the great secret of golf. You can't play a really hot game unless you're so miserable that you don't worry over your shots. . . . Look at the top-notchers. Have you ever seen a happy pro?"

P. G. WODEHOUSE

"Golf is not one of those occupations in which you soon learn your level. There is no shape nor size of body, no awkwardness nor ungainliness, which puts good golf beyond one's reach. There are good golfers with spectacles, with one eye, with one leg, even with one arm. None but the absolutely blind need despair. It is not the youthful tyro alone who has cause to hope. Beginners in middle age have become great, and, more wonderful still, after years of patient duffering, there may be a rift in the clouds. Some pet vice which has been clung to as a virtue may be abandoned, and the fifth-class player burst upon the world as a medal winner. In golf, whilst there is life there is hope."

SIR WALTER SIMPSON
from "The Art of Golf"

— ◆ —

O.LANDOLT

LUCERNE
AND
CENTRAL SWITZERLAND

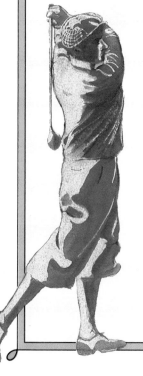

At the U.S. Open: "The person I fear most in the last two rounds is myself."

TOM WATSON

— ♦ —

"Reading a green is like reading the small type in a contract. If you don't read it with painstaking care, you are likely to be in trouble."

CLAUDE HAMILTON

— ♦ —

"Golf is more exacting than racing, cards, speculation or matrimony. Golf gives no margin: either you win or you fail. You cannot hedge; you cannot bluff; you cannot give a stop order. One chance is given you, and you hit or miss. There is nothing more rigid in life. And it is this ultra and extreme rigidity that makes golf so intensely interesting."

ARNOLD HAULTAIN, 1908

— ♦ —

"On the golf course, a man may be the dogged victim of inexorable fate, be struck down by an appalling stroke of tragedy, become the hero of unbelievable melodrama, or the clown in a side-splitting comedy - any of these within a few hours, and all without having to bury a corpse or repair a tangled personality."

ROBERT TYRE JONES

— ♦ —

"If your caddie coaches you on the tee, 'Hit it down the left side with a little draw,' ignore him. All you do on the tee is try not to hit the caddie."

JIM MURRAY

" 'I'm going to play Major G tomorrow,' said a member of the Royal and Ancient Golf Club to the old and experienced caddie he was employing, 'what sort of a player is he?' 'Oh, he canna play worth a damn,' answered the expert, 'he's nae better than yourself.' "

from "Told at the 19th Hole"

Shor, after shooting a 211:
What should I give the caddie?
Gleason: Your golf clubs.

TOOTS SHOR AND JACKIE GLEASON

Guide officiel

VILLARS, CHESIÈRES, ARVEYES, BRETAYE

Altitude: 1300-1800 m

Ligne du Simplon

La Perle des Stations de Montagne de la Suisse Romande

ADVICE FOR THE DUFFER

"The nice thing about these [golf] books is that they usually cancel each other out. One book tells you to keep your eye on the ball; the next says not to bother. Personally, in the crowd I play with, a better idea is to keep your eye on your partner."

JIM MURRAY
from "The Sporting World of Jim Murray"

— ♦ —

"The secret of missing a tree is to aim straight at it."

MICHAEL GREEN
from "The Art of Coarse Golf"

— ♦ —

"Always throw your clubs ahead of you. That way you don't have to waste energy going back to pick them up."

TOMMY BOLT

— ♦ —

"If the following foursome is pressing you, wave
them through and then speed up."
DEANE BEMAN

— ♦ —

"I see your golf is improving. You are missing
the ball much closer than you used to."
LEOPOLD FECHTNER
from "5,000 One- and Two-line Jokes"

Hope: Okay, what's wrong with my game?

Palmer: If you're talking about golf,

that's not your game.

ARNOLD PALMER and BOB HOPE. on NBC

"A Coarse Golfer is one who has to shout 'Fore' when he putts."

MICHAEL GREEN
from "The Art of Coarse Golf"

— ◆ —

"At least he can't cheat on his score - because all you have to do is look back down the fairway and count the wounded."

BOB HOPE

— ◆ —

"Golf acts as a corrective against sinful pride. I attribute the insane arrogance of the later Roman emperor almost entirely to the fact that, never having played golf, they never knew that strange chastening humility which is engendered by a topped chip shot."

P. G. WODEHOUSE

— ◆ —

"Golf has some drawbacks. It is possible, by too much of it, to destroy the mind. . . . For the golfer, Nature loses her significance. Larks, the casts of worms, the buzzing of bees, and even children are hateful. . . . Rain comes to be regarded solely in its relation to the putting greens; the daisy is detested, botanical specimens are but 'hazards', twigs 'break clubs'. Winds cease to be east, south, west or north. They are ahead, behind, or sideways, and the sky is bright or dark, according to the state of the game."

SIR WALTER SIMPSON, 1887

"A well-adjusted man is one who can play golf as if it were a game."

from "A Treasure Chest of Quotations"

"To get an elementary grasp of the game of golf, you must learn, by endless practice, a continuous and subtle series of highly unnatural movements, involving about sixty-four muscles, that result in a seemingly 'natural' swing, taking all of two seconds to begin and end."

ALISTAIR COOKE

"Everybody has two swings - a beautiful practice swing and the choked-up one with which they hit the ball.
So it wouldn't do either of us a damned bit of good to look at your practice swing."

ED FURGOL
from "Golf Magazine"

– ◆ –

GOLF
MONTE-CARLO

"Be funny on a golf course?
Do I kid my best friend's
mother about her heart condition?"

PHIL SILVERS
comedian

— ◆ —

"Golfers play golf to prove that they can
mentally overcome the pressures that golf puts
upon them. The fact that if they didn't play golf
at all they would not have to endure or
overcome its pressures may not occur to them."

PETER GAMMOND
from "Bluff Your Way in Golf"

— ◆ —

"He enjoys that perfect peace, that peace beyond
all understanding, which comes at its maximum
only to the man who has given up golf."

P. G. WODEHOUSE

— ◆ —

"To control his own ball, all alone without help or hindrance, the golfer must first and last entirely control himself, and himself only. The little round toy sitting so alone and so still, which has so fascinated and tantalized the human animal for more than five centuries, is thus uniquely a psychic as well as physical cynosure of muscular skill and mental concentration."

JOHN STUART MARTIN

"We speak of eyeball-to-eyeball encounters between men great and small. Even more searching and revealing of character is the eyeball-to-golfball confrontation, whereby our most secret natures are mercilessly tested by a small, round, whitish object with no mind or will but with a very definite life of its own, and with whims perverse and beatific."

JOHN STUART MARTIN

"I'd like to see the fairways more narrow. Then everybody would have to play from the rough, not just me."

SEVE BALLESTEROS

— ◆ —

IN THE ROUGH

"My goal this year is basically to find the fairways."

LAURI PETERSON
from "The San José Mercury News"

"Obviously a deer on the fairway has seen you tee off before and knows that the safest place to be when you play is right down the middle."

JACKIE GLEASON
to writer Milton Gross

"The hardest shot is a mashie at ninety yards from the green, where the ball has to be played against an oak tree, bounces back into a sandtrap, hits a stone, bounces on the green and then rolls into the cup. That shot is so difficult I have only made it once."

ZEPPO MARX

NOWHERE SO NAKED

"Golf is first a game of seeing and feeling. It can teach you stillness of mind and a sensitivity to the textures of wind and green. The best instructional books have always said this. Golf is also a game to teach you about the messages from within, about the subtle voices of the body-mind. And once you understand them you can more clearly see your 'harmartia', the ways in which your approach to the game reflects your entire life.

Nowhere does a person go so naked."

MICHAEL MURPHY

Sports d'Été et d'Hiver
Station d'altitude 1550 m. (5000 Feet)
MONTANA-VERMALA
s/SIERRE (SUISSE)

"Fluff: A shot in which the clubhead strikes the ground behind the ball before hitting it, causing it to dribble forward one or two yards. A more widely used term for this type of stroke is 'practice swing.' "

HENRY BEARD AND ROY MCKIE
from "Golfing - A Duffer's Dictionary"

— ◆ —

"I know I'm getting better at golf because I'm hitting fewer spectators."

GERALD R. FORD

— ◆ —

"I won't try to describe A.R.'s game, beyond saying the way he played it would have taken him three years of solid practice to work up to where he could be called a duffer."

PAUL GALLICO
from "Golf Is a Nice Friendly Game"

— ◆ —

"A professional will tell you the amount of flex you need in the shaft of your club. The more the flex, the more strength you will need to break the thing over your knees."

STEPHEN BAKER
from "How to Play Golf in the Low 120's"

$-\blacklozenge-$

"There are three ways of learning golf: by study, which is the most wearisome; by imitation, which is the most fallacious; and by experience, which is the most bitter."

ROBERT BROWNING
from "A History of Golf"

$-\blacklozenge-$

"The right way to play golf is to go up and hit the bloody thing."

GEORGE DUNCAN
Scottish professional

$-\blacklozenge-$

"Fairway: A narrow strip of mown grass that separates two groups of golfers looking for lost balls in the rough."

HENRY BEARD AND ROY MCKIE
from "Golfing - A Duffer's Dictionary"

— ◆ —

"When he gets the ball into a tough place, that's when he's most relaxed. I think it's because he has so much experience at it."

DON CHRISTOPHER
Jack Lemon's caddie'

— ◆ —

"My game is so bad I gotta hire three caddies -
one to walk the left rough, one for the right
rough, and one down the middle.
And the one in the middle doesn't
have much to do."

DAVE HILL
from "Golf Digest"

– ♦ –

"Wherein do the charms of this game lie, that captivate youth, and retain their hold till far on in life?... It is a fine, open-air, athletic exercise, not violent, but bringing into play nearly all the muscles of the body; while that exercise can be continued for hours. It is a game of skill, needing mind and thought and judgement, as well as a cunning hand. It is also a social game, where one may go out with one friend or with three, as the case may be, and enjoy mutual intercourse, mingled with an excitement which is very pleasing . . . It never palls or grows stale, as morning by morning the players appear at the teeing-ground with as keen a relish as if they had not seen a club for a month. Nor is it only while the game lasts that its zest is felt. How the player loves to recall the strokes and other incidents of the match, so that it is often played over again next morning while still in bed!"

JAMES BALFOUR, 1887

"Local Rules: A set of regulations that are ignored only by players on one specific course rather than by golfers as a whole."

HENRY BEARD AND ROY MCKIE
from "Golfing - A Duffer's Dictionary"

— ◆ —

"In competition, during gunfire or while bombs are falling, players may take cover without penalty for ceasing play.

The positions of known delayed-action bombs are marked by red flags at a reasonably, but not guaranteed, safe distance therefrom.... A ball moved by enemy action may be replaced, or if lost or 'destroyed' a ball may be dropped not nearer the hole without penalty. A player whose stroke is affected by the simultaneous explosion of a bomb may play another ball from the same place. Penalty, one stroke."

from "Temporary Rules, 1940, Richmond Golf Club"

THE PENNY
MAGAZINE

E LANDER

"It is a wonderful tribute to the game or to the dottiness of the people who play it that for some people somewhere there is no such thing as an insurmountable obstacle, an unplayable course, the wrong time of the day or year."

ALISTAIR COOKE

— ♦ —

"Indeed, the highest pleasure of golf may be that on the fairways and far from all the pressures of commerce and rationality, we can feel immortal for a few hours."

COLMAN McCARTHY
from "The Pleasures of the Game"

— ♦ —

"Eighteen holes of match play will teach you more about your foe than nineteen years of dealing with him across the desk."

GRANTLAND RICE

— ♦ —

ALTITUDE
1800m

GOLF DE HAUTE MONTAGNE

FONT-ROMEU

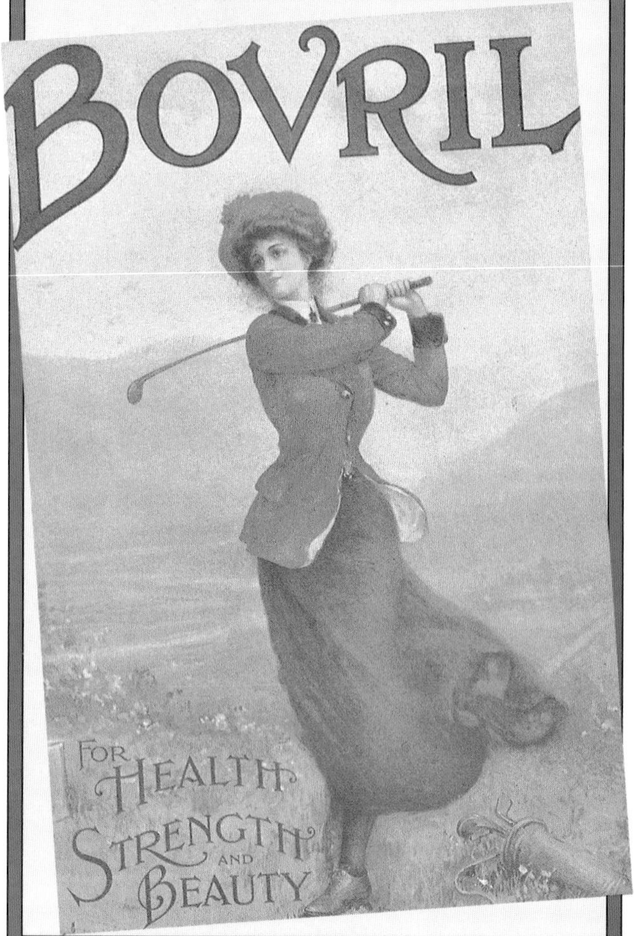
BOVRIL
FOR HEALTH
STRENGTH AND
BEAUTY

"Must you go off and play that wretched game again, darling? Leaving me here, alone and sad, to slave over the microwave oven?"

"Yes I must, I have promised to make up a four."

"Have you no regard for our marriage? Mother did warn me about golfers, but I never thought it could be like this."

"You are being very selfish. I must keep fit. And in any case the Club Trophy is next month and I am very out of practice."

"One day you will return to find me gone, the house empty, the children on the streets."

"Yes, well I must be going now. If we don't get off by two, it gets very crowded. I'll be back in time for supper."

And off she goes to the Club and he returns to the kitchen.

PETER GAMMOND
from "Bluff Your Way in Golf"

"One reward golf has given me, and I shall always be thankful for it, is introducing me to some of the world's most picturesque tireless and bald-faced liars."

REX LARDNER
from "Out of the Bunker and Into the Trees"

— ♦ —

"If you pick up a golfer and hold it close to your ear, like a conch shell, and listen - you will hear an alibi."

FRED BECK
from "89 Years in a Sand Trap"

— ♦ —

"Hole-in-One: An occurrence in which a ball is hit directly from the tee into the hole on a single shot by a golfer playing alone."

HENRY BEARD AND ROY MCKIE
from "Golfing - A Duffer's Dictionary"

— ♦ —

"It's still good sportsmanship to not pick up lost balls while they are still rolling."

MARK TWAIN

"There are now more golf clubs in the world than Gideon Bibles, more golf balls than missionaries and, if every golfer in the world, male and or female, were laid end to end, I for one would leave them there."

MICHAEL PARKINSON
the Anti-Golf Society,
from the "Sunday Times"

"True golfers do not play the game
as a form of stress management.
Quite the reverse. They play to
establish superiority over (a)
themselves, (b) inanimate objects
such as a small white ball with
dimples in it, and (c) their friends.
All of which can become rather
tedious."

COLIN BOWLES
from "The Cheat's Guide to Golf"

− ♦ −

"There is one thing in this world that is dumber
than playing golf. That is watching someone else
play golf. . . . What do you actually get to see?
Thirty-seven guys in polyester slacks squinting
at the sun. Doesn't that set your blood racing?"

PETER ANDREWS
from "Golf Digest"

− ♦ −

"FOOLS OUT OF EVERYBODY"

"**G**eorge, you look perfect. . .that beautiful knitted shirt, an alpaca sweater, those expensive slacks. . . .You've got an alligator bag, the finest matched irons, and the best woods money can buy. It's a damned shame you have to spoil it all by playing golf."

LLOYD MANGRUN
to the comedian, George Burns

"Golf does strange things to other people, too. It makes liars out of honest men, cheats out of altruists, cowards out of brave men and fools out of everybody."

MILTON GROSS
from "Eighteen Holes in My Head"

April 21 1927

Price 15 cents

Life

· SPORTS NUMBER ·

The Sport of Missing Men

"Golf is like a love affair: If you don't take it seriously, it's not fun; if you do take it seriously, it breaks your heart."

ARNOLD DALY

— ♦ —

"The fundamental problem with golf is that every so often, no matter how lacking you may be in the essential virtues required of a steady player, the odds are that one day you *will* hit the ball straight, hard and out of sight. This is the essential frustration of this excruciating sport. For when you've done it once, you make the fundamental error of asking yourself why you can't do it all the time. The answer to this question is simple: the first time was a fluke."

COLIN BOWLES
from "The Cheat's Guide to Golf"

— ♦ —

"If you watch a game, it's fun. If you play it, it's recreation. If you work at it, it's golf."

BOB HOPE

— ◆ —

"Real golfers go to work to relax."

GEORGE DILLON

— ◆ —

LES GOLFS
de la Côte Basque
et du Béarn

"No matter what happens - *never give up a hole*. . . .In tossing in your cards after a bad beginning you also undermine your whole game, because to quit between tee and green is more habit-forming than drinking a highball before breakfast."

SAM SNEAD

– ◆ –

"Don't let the bad shots get to you.
Don't let yourself become angry.
The true scramblers are thick-skinned.
And they always beat the whiners."

PAUL RUNYAN
from "Golf Digest"

– ◆ –

"In prehistoric times, cavemen had a custom of beating the ground with clubs and uttering spine-chilling cries. Anthropologists call this a form of primitive self-expression.
When modern men go through the same ritual, they call it golf."

ANON

"Anytime you get the urge to golf, instead take 18 minutes and beat your head against a good solid wall! This is guaranteed to duplicate to a tee the physical and emotional beating you would have suffered playing a round of golf. If 18 minutes aren't enough, go for 27 or 36 - whatever feels right."

MARK OMAN
from "Portrait of a Golfaholic"

Golf: "A game in which you claim the privileges of age, and retain the playthings of childhood."

SAMUEL JOHNSON